Lynyrd's

DAILY DOSE OF WIS-DUMB

Lynyrd's

DAILY DOSE OF WIS-DUMB

365 Wise Sayings from 1 Wise Guy

Written by John Bunn (AKA Lynyrd)
Layout and design by John Bunn
Design consultant: Jenny Bunn
Edited by Jenny Bunn
Printed by Amazon KDP
ISBN: 979-8-37-329416-4

LYNYRD

He's a man who's seen it all and understood very little of it. He wears his heart on his sleeve and taco sauce on his trousers. He needs no introduction but insists on having one, so here you go: He's the spotlight-stealin' country bumpkin who's as unpredictable as springtime in Ohio. He's the one-and-only (self-proclaimed) star of the the show at The Amish Country Theater in Berlin, Ohio. His name is **Lynyrd** and believe it or not, he writes books.

He's performed in Las Vegas, MGM Studios, on cruise ships, in barns and treehouses all over Ohio and he can been seen four nights a week at the world-famous Amish Country Theater.

IT'S LIKE THE MONDAY OF THE MONTHS.

JANUARY

1

Never kiss someone on January 1. You shouldn't kiss on the first date.

JANUARY

2

A New Year's resolution is something that goes in one year and out the other.

JANUARY

To truly find yourself,
play hide and seek alone.

JANUARY

Life is short. Smile while
you still have teeth.

JANUARY

If you want to marry a
professional athlete,
remember competitive
eating is a sport.

JANUARY

Some days you're the
pigeon. Other days
you're the statue.

JANUARY

A wise person doesn't get even. He only gets odder.

JANUARY

Two days from now, tomorrow will be yesterday.

JANUARY
9

May this morning's coffee
give you the strength to
make it to your mid-
morning coffee.

JANUARY
10

It's all fun and games
until your metabolism
slows down.

Never forget: you're
special and unique.
Just like everyone else.

Practice safe eating.
Always use condiments.

JANUARY

Friends are people who
know you well, but like
you anyway.

JANUARY

A wise husband always
thinks twice before
saying nothing.

JANUARY

15

Always proofread
carefully to make sure you
don't any words out.

JANUARY

16

Be nice to your friends.
Some day you might need
them to empty your bedpan.

The older you get,
the better you were.

If at first you don't succeed,
skydiving is not for you.

The easiest way to find
something that is lost:
Buy a replacement for it.

Inside every old person is a
young person wondering
what the heck happened.

JANUARY

21

Stop procrastinating—
starting tomorrow.

JANUARY

22

It would be ironic if you
died in the living room.

JANUARY

23

Marriage is that special
relationship that allows you to
annoy that one special person
for the rest of your life.

JANUARY

24

Never play leapfrog
with a unicorn.

JANUARY

25

If you're wrong and you shut
up, you're wise.
If you're right and you shut
up, you're married.

JANUARY

26

Never make the same mistake
twice. Make it three or four
times just to be sure.

JANUARY

27

He who throws dirt ...
loses ground.

JANUARY

28

A day without sunshine ...
is like night.

JANUARY

29

A waist is a terrible
thing to mind.

JANUARY
30

All men should freely use the seven words that have the power to make any marriage go smoothly: You know dear, you may be right.

JANUARY
31

Nachos are just tacos that don't have their life together.

CAN FEBRUARY MARCH?
NO, BUT APRIL MAY.

FEBRUARY

When someone yells, "STOP!", it can mean one of three things:

1. Time to smell the roses
2. Time to collaborate and listen
3. It's Hammer time

Groundhog Day: The day when Punxsutawney Phil sticks his head out of the ground and says, "Ok people, now it's really time to take down the Christmas decorations."

FEBRUARY
3

If you ever need a brain transplant, choose a teenager's. That way you'd get one that's never been used.

FEBRUARY
4

Half the people in the world are below average.

FEBRUARY

What I if told you ...
You read the top line wrong

FEBRUARY

Don't be ashamed of
who you are.
That's your parents' job.

FEBRUARY

Before you marry someone, make them use a computer with slow internet to find out who they really are.

FEBRUARY

If your parents never had children, chances are you won't either.

FEBRUARY

Those voices in your head
may not be real. But if you
listen hard enough, they do
have pretty awesome ideas.

FEBRUARY

Smoking will kill you.
Bacon will kill you. And yet,
smoking bacon will cure it.

FEBRUARY

If you ever get an email about pork, ham, salt, and preservatives ... don't open it. It's SPAM.

FEBRUARY

Eating a dictionary will give you thesaurus throat.

FEBRUARY
13

Worrying works.
99% of the things you worry
about never happen.

FEBRUARY
14

If two people love each other,
nothing is impossible ... except
deciding where to eat.

Farts are just ghosts of
the things we ate.

To avoid confusion, it's best
to give the kids and the
dogs different names.

FEBRUARY

Irony:
the opposite of wrinkly.

FEBRUARY

Whatever you do, always
give 100% ... unless you're
giving blood.

FEBRUARY

There are two rules in life:
1. Never give out all the
information.

FEBRUARY

If everyone tells you to
follow your dreams ...
go back to bed.

21

If we're not supposed to have midnight snacks, why is there a light in the fridge?

22

You never realize how long a minute is until you exercise.

23

The next time your wife gets angry, drape a towel over her shoulders (like a cape) and say, "Now you're SUPER ANGRY!" Maybe she'll laugh. Maybe you'll die.

Parents: people who tell you not to believe everything you see on the internet, but believe everything they see on Facebook.

FEBRUARY

25

Just be happy.
It drives people crazy.

FEBRUARY

26

The police never think it's
as funny as you do.

FEBRUARY

27

If at first you DO succeed,
try to hide your astonishment.

FEBRUARY

28

Some people walk into our
lives and leave footprints on
our hearts. Others walk into
our lives and we want to leave
footprints on their face!

FEBRUARY

29

LEAP DAY BONUS!

Save business cards of people you don't like. If you ever hit a parked car, write "sorry" on the back and leave it on the windshield.

GONNA HAVE TO MARCH
FOR 31 LOOOOONG DAYS

MARCH

1

Name your dog "Five Miles" so
you can tell people you walk
Five Miles every day.

MARCH

2

If you follow my rules, you
will never lose money.
Rule #1: Never lose money.

MARCH

3

If you think no one cares
you're alive ... try missing
a couple car payments.

MARCH

4

Velcro shoes are a
total rip off.

MARCH

When you are stressed,
eat ice cream, cake,
and chocolate because
stressed spelled
backwards is desserts.

MARCH

Is the glass half empty,
half full, or just twice as
big as it needs to be?

MARCH
7

Saying "super size it" works at McDonald's but not at the pharmacy.

MARCH
8

Red meat is not bad for you. Fuzzy green meat is bad for you.

MARCH

Not everyone ages like fine wine. Some age like milk. They get sour and chunky.

MARCH

If you can sleep like a baby, you probably don't have one.

MARCH

If life gives you lemons,
squirt someone in the eye.

MARCH

If life gives you melons,
you're probably dyslexic.

People are like
refrigerators. It's what's on
the inside that matters.

A wise doctor once wrote:

MARCH

15

If you go to bed at night
wondering where the sun went,
eventually it will dawn on you.

MARCH

16

Snack often so your
kitchen doesn't get lonely
between meals.

45

MARCH

Never iron a four-leaf clover. You don't want to press your luck.
Happy St. Patrick's Day!

MARCH

Whoever said "Out of sight, out of mind" never had a spider disappear in their bedroom.

MARCH

19

Whoever said patience is a virtue never had to surf the web without high-speed Internet.

MARCH

20

Those who stand on toilets are high on pot.

MARCH

21

In the spring, birds return from their tropical vacation. Six months later they regret their decision and go back.

MARCH

22

4 out of 3 people struggle with math.

Change your name on Facebook to "Nobody," so when you see someone posting something stupid you can like their post and it will say "Nobody likes this."

24

The toughest part of a
diet isn't watching what
you eat ... it's watching
what other people eat.

25

Yawning is the body's way
of telling you it has only
15% battery remaining.

If someone is laughing, laugh with them. If someone is singing, sing with them. If someone is working, let them work... you don't want to ruin their concentration.

MARCH

27

You never realize how many people you don't like until you have to name a baby.

MARCH

28

You are one step away from being rich. All you need now is money.

29

Denial, anger, bargaining, depression, and acceptance: The five stages of waking up.

30

The best way to show a giraffe your love is to knit a scarf for it.

Pro Tip: In the event of a tornado or other such natural disaster, place wieners and/or cheese slices in your pockets so the search dogs can find you first.

**PRANK YOU.
PRANK YOU VERY MUCH.**

APRIL
1

Today is April Fools' Day.
Believe nothing and trust no one.
(Just like any other day.)

APRIL
2

Fool me once, shame on you. Fool
me twice, shame on me. Fool me
three times ... you're good at this
and I can respect that.

APRIL
3

If you sneeze without a
tissue, you take matters into
your own hands.

APRIL
4

Remember, if the world
didn't suck, we'd all fall off.

APRIL
5

Rabbits jump and they live for 8 years. Dogs run and they live for 15 years. Turtles do nothing and live for 150 years. Lesson learned.

APRIL
6

Eat more donuts.
They're the original hole foods.

APRIL

7

One big difference between men and women is that if a woman says, "Smell this," it usually smells nice.

APRIL

8

Nutrition labels should include a "What if I ate the whole thing" section.

Success isn't always as rewarding as it seems. Caesar was the greatest emperor who ever lived and all they did was name a salad after him.

10

If Facebook has taught us anything it's that a lot of people aren't quite ready for a spelling bee.

11

Dinosaurs never had coffee, and we see how that turned out.

APRIL

12

If you don't cut the pizza in pieces and just eat the whole pizza, then you only had one piece.

APRIL

13

He who laughs at himself never runs out of things to laugh at.

14

Life's three unwritten rules:

1.

2.

3.

Just because children are deductible, it doesn't mean they aren't taxing.

Some people are such treasures, you just want to bury them.

APRIL

17

The best way to hang up on someone is when you are in the middle of your own sentence. That way they never suspect you hung up on them.

APRIL

18

When your dreams turn to dust, it's time to vacuum.

APRIL

19

When you're young, you sneak out of the house to go to parties. When you're old, you sneak out of parties to go home.

APRIL

20

Eat cake. It's somebody's birthday somewhere.

APRIL
21

If you don't watch cable news, you're uninformed. If you watch cable news, you're misinformed.

APRIL
22

Behind every angry woman is a man who has absolutely no idea what he did wrong.

APRIL
23

Some people are like glow sticks. You wish you could snap them and shake them real hard until the light comes on.

APRIL
24

If your nose goes on strike ... picket.

APRIL

25

In this day and age, no need
to ask people what they like
to do in their free time.
It's Netflix.
We all just watch Netflix.

APRIL

26

Of all your body parts, your
fingers are the most reliable.
You can always count on them.

APRIL
27

You never see anyone jogging and smiling. So that's all you need to know about that.

APRIL
28

The worst time to have a heart attack is during a game of charades.

Don't be afraid to try something new. An amateur built the ark. It lasted forty days and forty nights. Professionals built the Titanic. It sank on the fourth day.

You're riding a horse full speed and there's a giraffe on your left and a lion right behind you. What do you do?

Get off the carousel.

**APRIL SHOWERS BRING MAY FLOWERS.
MAY FLOWERS BRING ... ALLERGIES.**

MAY

1

If you don't finish the
things you start, you'll
earn a blackbelt in
partial arts.

MAY

2

If you ever get the
opportunity to use a
telescope, you should
definitely look into it.

MAY

3

Friends come and friends go
like the waves of the ocean.
But a true friend stays like an
octopus on your face.

MAY

4

May the Fourth be with you.

MAY

5

If you had to choose between eating tacos every day or being thin for the rest of your life, would you choose hard or soft tacos?

Happy Cinco De Mayo!

MAY

6

I always found it a little ironic
when a teacher would say,
"Don't get smart with me."

MAY

7

Hard work pays off in
the future. Laziness pays
off right now.

MAY

Mother's Day is coming. Be sure to remind your mom to have all the cleaning and laundry done by Saturday evening so she can enjoy her special day.

MAY

Yeah, abs are great ...
but have you tried donuts?

MAY

10

The trick is to not let people know how weird you really are until it's too late for them to back out.

MAY

11

Laughter is the best medicine ... unless you have diarrhea.

MAY

12

One way to find out if you're old
is to fall down in front of a
crowd. If they laugh at you,
you're still young. If they run to
you concerned, you're getting old.

MAY

13

You can't be late if
you never show up.

MAY

14

Don't worry about biting off more than you can chew. Your mouth is probably a whole lot bigger than you think.

MAY

15

There are two ingredients in trail mix: M&Ms and disappointment.

MAY
16

You know that tingly little feeling you get with you like someone? That is common sense leaving your body.

MAY
17

You don't need a hairstylist. Your pillow will give you a new hair style every morning.

MAY
18

Start dreaming of a better
world, where chickens can
cross the road without anyone
questioning their motives.

MAY
19

Don't steal.
That's the government's job.

MAY
20

Never step on a Froot Loop.
It'll make you a cereal killer.

MAY
21

Some days you eat salads and
go to the gym. Some days you
eat cupcakes and refuse to put
on pants. It's called balance.

MAY
22

Being an adult is like folding a
fitted sheet. No one really
knows how to do it.

MAY
23

Don't blame others for
the road you're on.
That's your own asphalt.

MAY

24

Right before you die, swallow
a bag of popcorn kernels.
Your cremation will be epic.

MAY

25

If you love someone, let
them go. If they come
back with coffee,
it was meant to be.

MAY

26

When everything's coming your way, you're probably in the wrong lane.

MAY

27

If you want to look young and thin, hang out with old and fat people.

MAY

28

People who wonder if the glass is half full or half empty miss the point. The glass is refillable.

MAY

29

If the grass is greener on the other side, you can bet that their water bill is higher.

When a woman says she'll be ready in five minutes, think like five minutes left in the fourth quarter and both teams have all of their timeouts.

Everybody wants to be the goat. But goats jump around randomly, eat whatever they want, and head-butt anyone who annoys them.

Don't be the goat.

... NAH, NAH, NAH, NAH ...
HEY JUNE

JUNE
1

If a man says he'll fix it, he'll fix it. No need to nag him about it every six months.

JUNE
2

It makes no sense to depend on a rabbit's foot for good luck. It obviously didn't work for the rabbit.

JUNE

3

If you want to get a job in the lotion industry, the best advice is to apply daily.

JUNE

4

If you go to bed and dream about being a muffler, you'll always wake up exhausted.

JUNE
5

This too shall pass. It may pass like a massive kidney stone, but it will pass.

JUNE
6

You never realize how little self-control you have until you're at a Mexican restaurant and the chips and salsa are in front of you.

JUNE

7

Don't ever let anyone accuse you of lollygagging when you are, in fact, dilly-dallying.

JUNE

8

Life was much simpler when we could play Red Rover and just clothesline people we didn't like.

JUNE
9

Our eyes water when we yawn
because we miss our bed.
And it makes us sad.

JUNE
10

Nothing screws up your
Friday like realizing
it's only Wednesday.

If you don't know the
difference between
"there" "their" and
"they're" your an idiot.

Everybody wants to
change the world. But
nobody wants to change
the toilet paper roll.

JUNE

13

It's okay to fall apart
sometimes. Tacos do.
And we still love them.

JUNE

14

The secret to success is
sincerity. Once you can fake
that, you've got it made.

JUNE
15

He who laughs last
probably didn't get the
joke in the first place.

JUNE
16

A recent study showed that
women who carry a little
extra weight live longer than
the men who mention it.

JUNE
17

You can tell a lot about a woman's mood by looking at her hands. For instance, if they are holding a gun, she's probably angry.

JUNE
18

Never ask a barber if you need a haircut.

JUNE
19

A bed is that magical
place where you suddenly
remember everything you
forgot to do.

JUNE
20

A papercut is a tree's
final moment of revenge.

JUNE
21

When life closes a door,
just open it again. It's a
door. That's how they work.

JUNE
22

Common sense is like
deodorant. Those who need
it most never use it.

JUNE

23

People say you can't live
without love. But I think
oxygen is more important.

JUNE

24

Lies are like bald spots. The
bigger they are, the harder
it is to cover it up.

JUNE
25

It's funny how people get mad when a sentence doesn't end the way chicken nuggets.

JUNE
26

Diet tip: Your pants can never get too tight if you don't wear any.

JUNE

27

Facebook needs three buttons: "Like," "Dislike," and "Stop Being Stupid."

JUNE

28

Tomorrow you will break your personal record for most days lived.

JUNE

29

Childhood injuries: Fell off my bike, fell out of a tree, sprained my ankle.
Adult injuries: Slept wrong, got up too fast, sneezed too hard.

JUNE

30

If someone's hotter than you it means you're cooler than them.

CRAP! THAT'S DUE TOMORROW?

- THOMAS JEFFERSON, JULY 3, 1776 (PROBABLY)

JULY

1

The hardest thing you'll ever do: waiting until the movie starts to eat your popcorn.

JULY

2

If you break a bone in two places, stop going to those places.

JULY

3

The easiest way to organize your stuff is to get rid of most of it.

JULY

4

Remember kids, don't play with fireworks. Let the adults who've been drinking all day do it. Happy Independence Day!

JULY
5

It's amazing how much the word "exercise" sounds like "extra fries."

JULY
6

Better to keep your mouth shut and look stupid than to open it and prove it.

JULY

7

If you wait long enough
to make dinner, everyone
will eventually eat
cereal. It's science.

JULY

8

If you eat something and
nobody sees you eat it, it
has no calories.

JULY

9

You don't need to be faster
than the bear. You just need
to be faster than the slowest
guy running from the bear.

JULY

10

78% of arguments
start because someone
hasn't eaten yet.

JULY

11

You know you're old when people start telling you how young you look.

JULY

12

Ladies, if he can't appreciate fruit jokes ... you need to let that mango.

JULY
13

Some people need a
speed bump between their
brains and their mouths.

JULY
14

Don't tell secrets in the
garden. The potatoes have
eyes. The corn has ears.
And the beanstalk.

JULY
15

If you had a DeLorean,
you could drive it from
time to time.

JULY
16

No man knows true happiness
until he gets married. By
then, of course, it's too late.

JULY

17

When all is said and done,
more is said than done.

JULY

18

Never go skinny dipping
with snapping turtles.

JULY

19

When all else fails,
read the instructions.

20

Good health is merely
the slowest possible way
a person can die.

21

Marriage tip: your wife will
never start a fight with you
while you're cleaning.

JULY

22

Growing up, bedtime was 9 pm. I couldn't wait to be an adult so I could go to bed when I wanted. Turns out it's 9 pm.

JULY

23

Work eight hours, sleep eight hours; just not the same eight hours.

JULY
24

We come from dust and we'll return to dust. That's why you shouldn't dust. It could be someone you know.

JULY
25

If at first you don't succeed, try using duct tape.

JULY

26

Did you know? Alligators can live to be 100 years old; which literally increases the chances that they will, indeed, see you later.

JULY

27

Forgive your enemies.
It messes with their heads.

JULY

28

Turning vegan would
be a big missed steak.

JULY

29

Sometimes in life,
you just need to see
things from a different
perspective.

JULY
30

Until you walk a mile in another person's shoes ... you can't imagine the smell.

JULY
31

The day is coming when your brain will go from, "You probably shouldn't say that," to, "What the heck, let's see what happens."

THE LAST HOT, SWEATY MONTH STANDING BETWEEN YOU AND PUMPKIN SPICE SEASON.

AUGUST

1

Due to inflation, the five second rule has been extended to ten seconds.

AUGUST

2

I don't always WHOOP. But when I do ...

There it is.

AUGUST

If you paint your truck camo, you can hunt without ever leaving your vehicle.

AUGUST

Pro tip: keep a cake moist by eating it all in one sitting.

AUGUST

Birthdays are good for your health. Studies show that people who have more birthdays live the longest.

AUGUST

One advantage of talking to yourself is at least you know someone's listening.

AUGUST

Never pick a fight with an
old man. If he is too old to
fight, he'll just kill you.

AUGUST

You never know what you
have until it's gone.
Toilet paper, for example.

AUGUST

Autocorrect can go
straight to he'll.

AUGUST

Tip of the day: Replace
your cat's litter box with a
Fed-Ex box. Then when it
gets full, tape it shut and
put it on the front porch
for someone to steal.

AUGUST

If you keep your head in the
clouds, your feet on the
ground, and keep reaching for
the stars, eventually you'll
need to see a chiropractor.

AUGUST

It takes guts to be
an organ donor.

AUGUST

You can reduce your chances of being bitten by a shark by 50% when you go swimming with a friend.

AUGUST

If you DO get bitten by a shark, bite it back. You'll probably still die but the shark will be like, "LOL what?"

AUGUST
15

You can't make everybody happy. You aren't a jar of Nutella.

AUGUST
16

Do NOT read the next sentence. You little rebel. I like you.

AUGUST
17

Respect your parents.
They made it through school
without Google.

AUGUST
18

True friends don't care if
your house is dirty.
They care if you have coffee.

AUGUST

Some people just need a high five. In the face. With a chair.

AUGUST

If someone makes you take off your shoes when you enter their house, take a better pair when you leave.

AUGUST
21

Men should do all
the coffee-making.
The Bible says: HE-BREWS.

AUGUST
22

If you are lucky enough to
find a weirdo you can call
your own, never let them go.

AUGUST
23

You're not overweight.
You're kidnap resistant.

AUGUST
24

Instead of calling your
bathroom "the John," rename
it "the Jim." That way you
can tell people you go to
the Jim every morning.

AUGUST
25

The main function of the little toe on your foot is to make sure that all your furniture is in the right place.

AUGUST
26

True friends don't judge each other, they judge other people ... together.

AUGUST

27

Nothing tops a plain pizza.

AUGUST

28

It's a good thing farting isn't contagious like yawning is.

AUGUST

29

Lif is too short.

AUGUST

30

Never go to bed angry.
Stay up and plot your revenge.

AUGUST

31

Pobody's nerfect.

BA-DEE-YA, SAY, DO YOU REMEMBER?
BA-DEE-YA, DANCIN' IN SEPTEMBER?
ADMIT IT, YOU SANG THAT AS YOU READ IT.

SEPTEMBER

1

When a cookie falls to the
floor and you bend down to
pick it, you better believe
that counts as a squat!

SEPTEMBER

2

Never discuss your pan pizza.
It's personal.

SEPTEMBER
3

Don't worry if you forget
how a boomerang works.
Eventually it will come
back to you.

SEPTEMBER
4

Invest in penny stocks.
It makes a lot of cents.

SEPTEMBER

Try this the next time a telemarketer calls: Answer the phone and say, "Hello caller, you're on the air!"

SEPTEMBER

A conclusion is simply the place where your brain got tired of thinking.

SEPTEMBER

If you ever get addicted to
the Hokey Pokey, don't
worry. Eventually you'll
turn yourself around.

SEPTEMBER

Taking a dog named Shark
to the beach is a bad idea.

SEPTEMBER

You can trust your dog to
guard your house but never
trust your dog to guard
your sandwich.

SEPTEMBER

Less is more, unless it's
kindness, sleep ...
or toilet paper.

SEPTEMBER

The easiest way to burn 2,000 calories: Fall asleep with brownies in the oven.

SEPTEMBER

The first 40 years of childhood are the hardest.

Even The Grinch had a dog.
So if you don't like dogs,
you may need to do some
soul-searching.

Passing gas on an elevator is
wrong on so many levels.

SEPTEMBER

Today is national
camouflage day.
Don't let anyone
see you celebrating.

SEPTEMBER

One place you can always find
love: Webster's Dictionary,
page 383, bottom left.

Don't be so hard on sharks.
If a stranger came into my
house wearing only a Speedo,
I'd probably get angry too.

Eating prunes will give you a
good run for your money.

No matter how good the hand soap smells, never walk out of the restroom sniffing your fingers.

If you eat crackers in bed, you will wake up feeling crumby.

SEPTEMBER
21

Scientists say that the universe
is made up of protons,
neutrons, and electrons.
They failed to mention morons.

SEPTEMBER
22

Smile. It will either warm
their heart or tick them off.
Either way, you win!

SEPTEMBER

23

Marriage tip: don't ask your wife what time dinner will be ready while she is mowing the lawn.

SEPTEMBER

24

When you see someone crying, ask if it's because of their haircut.

SEPTEMBER

25

Try resistance training.
Refuse to go to the gym.

SEPTEMBER

26

The older you get,
the earlier it gets late.

SEPTEMBER

27

Life Hack: If you sleep until lunch time, you can save breakfast money.

SEPTEMBER

28

Men: never laugh at your wife's choices. You are one of them.

SEPTEMBER
29

The worst part about losing
your glasses is that you don't
have your glasses to help you
look for your glasses.

SEPTEMBER
30

The best way to avoid
being stressed at work
is not going to work.

IT'S OCTOBER AND THAT MEANS HALLOWEEN WHICH BASICALLY MEANS THANKSGIVING THEN THAT BASICALLY MEANS CHRISTMAS. MERRY CHRISTMAS!

Never let anyone treat you like a yellow Starburst. You are a PINK Starburst, baby!

Life is too short for fake butter, fake cheese, and fake people.

OCTOBER
3

Face it: there will be days
when you feel as useless as
the G in lasagna.

OCTOBER
4

Birds of a feather flock
together ... and almost always
poop on your car.

OCTOBER

5

Geology rocks. But geography is where it's at.

OCTOBER

6

Some things are better left unsaid. You generally realize that right after you've said them.

OCTOBER

When someone says, "Expect
the unexpected," slap them
and say, "You didn't expect
that, did you?"

OCTOBER

Fun-size candy bars
aren't as fun after you've
had 43 of them.

OCTOBER

Don't be so hard on yourself. The mom in E.T. had an alien living in her house for days and didn't even notice.

OCTOBER

Invite people over regularly. It'll force you to clean your house.

OCTOBER

October is too early to have
your Christmas lights up ...
Unless they're still up from
last Christmas.

OCTOBER

A woman's mind is cleaner
than a man's. That's because
she changes it more often.

OCTOBER
13

When something in your life
goes wrong just yell,
"Plot twist!" and move on.

OCTOBER
14

How to parallel park:
Step 1. Park somewhere else.

OCTOBER
15

Silence is golden.
Unless you have kids.
Then silence is suspicious.

OCTOBER
16

Mirrors can't talk.
Fortunately they
can't laugh either.

OCTOBER

17

Buttcheeks is actually two
words. You should spread
them apart.

OCTOBER

18

If you can't laugh at your
own problems, call me and
I'll laugh at them.

OCTOBER
19

Cell phones keep getting
thinner and smaller.
People ... not so much.

OCTOBER
20

If you think nothing is
impossible, try slamming
a revolving door.

21

On Mercury, a day lasts 1,408 hours. Same as a Monday on Earth.

22

If at first you don't succeed, do it the way she told you in first place.

OCTOBER
23

Families are like fudge.
Mostly sweet with a few
nuts mixed in.

OCTOBER
24

You're not crazy. Just ask
your imaginary friends.

OCTOBER

25

The first five days after the
weekend are always tough.

OCTOBER

26

If you're too open-mined,
your brains may fall out.

OCTOBER

27

Death is hereditary.

OCTOBER

28

Doing nothing is hard.
You never know when
you're finished.

OCTOBER

29

Find someone who looks at
you the way you look at
chocolate cake.

OCTOBER
30

If one door closes and
another one opens, your
house is probably haunted.

OCTOBER
31

If zombies ever attack, just go to
Costco. They have strong walls,
years of food supply, and zombies
can't get in because they don't
have a membership card.

**MOVE OVER SPOOKY STUFF.
IT'S TURKEY TIME!**

NOVEMBER

1

Never trust a set of stairs.
They're always up to
something.

NOVEMBER

2

When you're single you
want to change the world.
Once you're married, you
can't even change the
channel on the TV.

NOVEMBER
3

The secret to having a
long marriage:
Never get divorced.

NOVEMBER
4

Not all fairytales begin
with, "Once upon a time..."
Many of them begin with,
"If elected, I promise..."

NOVEMBER

Life isn't about the moments that take your breath away. That's asthma. You're thinking of asthma.

NOVEMBER

The problem with political jokes is that they sometimes get elected.

NOVEMBER

Mind your own biscuits
and life will be gravy.

NOVEMBER

Stress balls are not for
throwing at people who
stress you out.

NOVEMBER

Rhinos are just
fat unicorns.

NOVEMBER

You have to be odd
to be number one.

NOVEMBER

Almost everything will work
if you unplug it for a few
minutes. That includes you.

NOVEMBER

I want buns of steel. But I
also want buns of cinnamon.

NOVEMBER
13

Friday the 13th is still
better than Monday the
whatever.

NOVEMBER
14

Eagles soar. But weasels
never get sucked into
jet engines.

NOVEMBER

When our phones fall,
we panic. When our
friends fall, we laugh.

NOVEMBER

Good moms let you lick
the beaters. Great moms
turn them off first.

NOVEMBER

With great power comes an
even greater electric bill.

NOVEMBER

Love may be blind, but
marriage is a real eye-opener.

NOVEMBER

When you have a bladder infection, urine trouble.

NOVEMBER

You have no one to blame but yourself. Unless some other guy is standing next to you. Then you can blame him.

Do lunges to stay in shape.
They're a big step forward.

There are three ways to get
something done:
do it yourself, hire someone,
or forbid your kids to do it.

NOVEMBER

23

Happy Thanksgiving!
Remember to set your
scales back ten pounds
this weekend.

NOVEMBER

24

If you get Hungary,
Russian to the kitchen and
Czech the fridge.

NOVEMBER
25

Stay away from sushi.
It seems a little fishy.

NOVEMBER
26

The early bird gets the worm.
You should just sleep until
the pancakes are ready.

NOVEMBER

27

One day you're the greatest thing since sliced bread. The next day, you're toast.

NOVEMBER

28

Never take a laxative and a sleeping pill at the same time.

NOVEMBER

29

It's impossible to say,
"Good eye might," without
sounding Australian.

NOVEMBER

30

To err is human.
To arr is pirate.

DEAR SANTA, JUST LEAVE YOUR CREDIT CARD UNDER THE TREE.

DECEMBER

Science has yet to explain how 300 people can be working at Walmart but only two check-out lanes will be open.

DECEMBER

Mountains aren't just funny. They're hill areas.

DECEMBER

When a woman says "What?"
it's not because she didn't hear
you. She's giving you a chance
to change what you said.

DECEMBER

If you have a bad cough,
take laxatives. Then you will
be afraid to cough.

DECEMBER

They say that love is more
important than money.
But have you ever tried to pay
your bills with a hug?

DECEMBER

Spilling hot coffee on your
lap wakes you up faster
than drinking it.

DECEMBER

Don't forget to drink water and get some sun. You're basically a houseplant with more complicated emotions.

DECEMBER

Never tell a woman she's crazy ... unless you want to SEE crazy.

9

Unless you fell while you were on the treadmill, nobody wants to hear about your workout.

10

Drinking coffee in the morning helps others live longer.

DECEMBER

If you're being chased by a
pack of taxidermists,
do NOT play dead.

DECEMBER

If you want to impress
me with your car, it
better be a food truck.

DECEMBER

Always remember to be nice
to people who have access to
your toothbrush.

DECEMBER

Don't believe everything
you think.

Santa should publish his naughty list. What a great way to meet people.

Why be moody when you can shake your booty?

Be the kind of person your
dog thinks you are.

A wise man always remembers
a woman's birthday but never
remembers her age.

Don't allow statistics to do
a number on you.

DECEMBER
20

With the rise of self-driving
vehicles, it's only a matter of
time until we get a country
song where a guy's truck
leaves him, too.

DECEMBER
21

A balanced diet:
A cupcake in each hand.

DECEMBER

22

Adulthood is like losing your parents in the supermarket for the rest of your life.

DECEMBER

23

Never ask a starfish for directions.

DECEMBER
24

For what it's worth: you
rarely see someone crying
and eating a Christmas
cookie at the same time.

DECEMBER
25

The Grinch never hated
Christmas. He hated people
... which is fair.

DECEMBER
26

Don't blame the holidays.
You were fat in August.

DECEMBER
27

If you're looking for a wise
investment, buy a barn.
It's a stable business.

The three hardest
things to say are:

1. I'm sorry
2. I was wrong
3. Worcestershire sauce

29

When someone tells you,
"You're going to regret that
in the morning," Just sleep
until noon. Problem solved.

30

Boomerangs and attention
deficit disorder do not mix.

DECEMBER

31

When driving keep your hands on the wheel, your eyes on the road, and your head out of your apps.

Check out Lynyrd's other books:

Y'know What I Meme

Laughing With Lynyrd

available on amazon.com

Made in the USA
Columbia, SC
17 February 2023

12491771R00126